A REGULAR FLOOD OF MISHAP

by Tom Birdseye

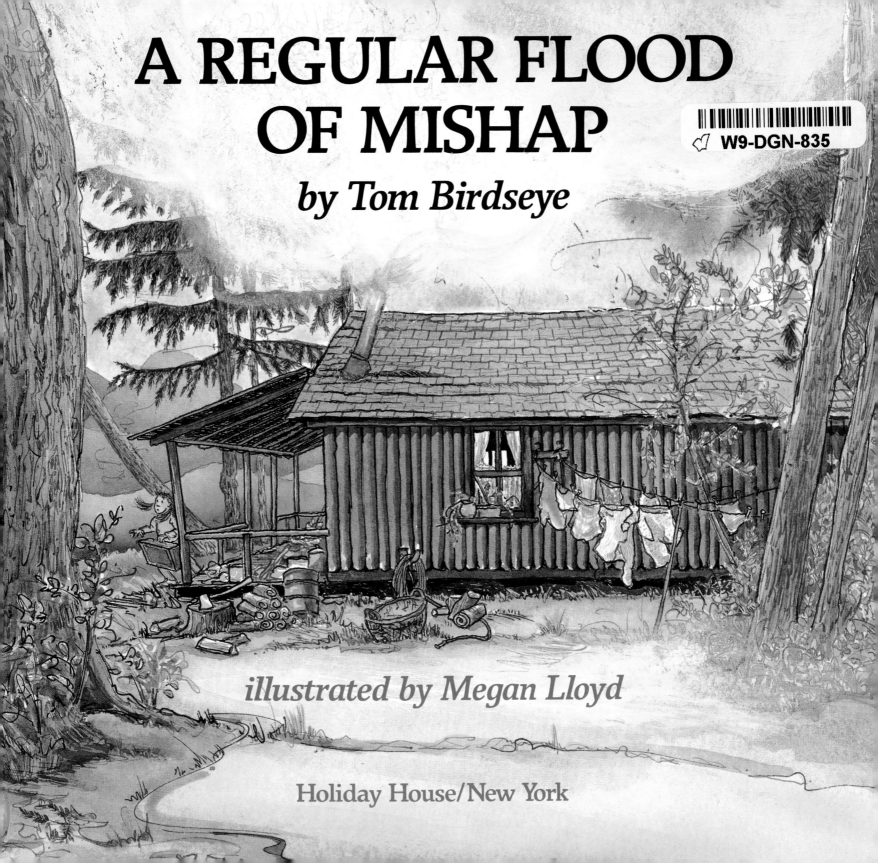

illustrated by Megan Lloyd

Holiday House/New York

For Mom, who put up with a
regular flood of mishap raising me.
T.B.

For the Quirks, a flood of fun.
M.L.

Text copyright © 1994 by Tom Birdseye
Illustrations copyright © 1994 by Megan Lloyd
ALL RIGHTS RESERVED
Printed in the United States of America

Library of Congress Cataloging-in-Publication Data
Birdseye, Tom.
A regular flood of mishap / by Tom Birdseye ;
illustrated by Megan Lloyd. — 1st ed.
p.   cm.
Summary: Six-year-old Ima Bean sets off such a "flood of mishaps"
when she tries to help her grandpa that she begins to worry whether
she will ever be forgiven.
ISBN 0-8234-1070-6
[1. Country life—Fiction.   2. Family life—Fiction.   3. Humorous
stories.]   I. Lloyd, Megan, ill.   II. Title.
PZ7.B5213Re   1994   93-9888   CIP   AC
[E]—dc20
ISBN 0-8234-1338-1 (pbk.)

I've lived here on Mossyrock Creek all my life—six years—but now I'm leaving for good.

Uh huh. It's true. My name is Ima Bean, and you heard me right. I've packed that old suitcase Aunt Etta Bean gave me last Christmas, and I'm skedaddling out of here as fast as a frog off a hot frying pan. Because my family doesn't love me anymore. And I can't blame 'em. You see . . . I goofed.

I didn't mean to make such a terrible mess, though! I was just trying to help.

It all started when I was down by the creek and spied
Grandpaw Bean's fishing pole propped up on a rock. Why, Ima
Bean! I said to myself. Grandpaw Bean has gone off and
plumb forgotten his fishing pole.

So I ran on over and picked that pole up.

Wouldn't ya know! Grandpaw Bean had plumb forgotten his
fishing line, too. It was still dangling in the water like it had
nothing else to do.

Better take that line to him as well, Ima Bean, I said to myself. (I was just trying to help.) A fishing pole's not much more
than a long stick without it, now is it?

So I commenced to reeling that line in.

Wouldn't ya know! Grandpaw Bean had plumb forgotten he had a hook tied to the end of that line, and it sure seemed snagged.

So I took a good hold of Grandpaw Bean's pole. And I cranked. And I yanked.

But that hook just refused to come loose.

Wouldn't ya know! Grandpaw Bean had plumb forgotten about that big log on the creek bottom. I reckoned his fishing hook was stuck in that thing as sure as pigs like mud.

Ima Bean, this calls for a little more *umph*, I said to myself. (I was just trying to help.)

So I put my feet up against a big rock. And I took a big breath. And I closed my eyes real tight. And I heaved. And I hauled. And I grunted like a big old fat hog.

And then I gave one big huge-o-mongous pull.

And directly I heard something hit the water.

And I opened up my eyes.
And discovered it was me!
Water was everywhere right about then, I noticed, coming
up to way over my head.

So spittin' and sputterin', grumblin' and mutterin', I swam to shore and climbed up on the bank, dragging Grandpaw Bean's fishing line behind me.

Wouldn't ya know! That line wasn't stuck in a big log like I'd thought it was. Grandpaw Bean had plumb forgotten he had some bait on that hook of his. He'd gone and caught himself a BIG old catfish.

Heavens to Bean, Ima! I said to myself. You'd better get that fish on home for fixin'. (I was just trying to help.) Grandpaw Bean will be as excited as a fly at a marmalade picnic when he sees this. Catfish. Mmmmm! Yahoodyhoo!

But then I saw Grandpaw Bean's fishing pole, broke in two.

Dear me. Oh my. Black clouds fly my troubles in the sky. I'd goofed.

So I ran home real quick to get a piece of string to try and tie that fishing pole back together.

Wouldn't ya know! I'd plumb forgotten that my daddy (people around Mossyrock Creek know him as Garbanzo Bean) had wrapped that string real tight around the barnyard gate for a reason—to keep it closed. When I untied it, the gate swung open, and out galloped Hester the mule like kids at Christmas. Right through the clothesline he went, dragging it and Mama Lima Bean's wash behind him.

"I'll get him, Daddy! Don't cry, Mama!" I yelled. (I was just trying to help.) "Whoa, Hester! Whoa!"

But Hester didn't whoa.

So I grabbed Brother Chili Bean's
bicycle to help chase that mule down.

Wouldn't ya know! I'd plumb forgotten that the front tire of Chili's bicycle
needed a new whatchamacallit, or a
whatchama*other*callit from when he'd
run it into the pig trough. I got no more
than one foot shy of two feet going when that front wheel
came off that bike and took off on its own like it had a pre-
vious engagement. I was thrown face foremost into the cabbages and carrots and 'taters and 'maters Mama had piled in
the garden cart.

Which then began to roll.

"But I was just trying to help!" I yelled as that fast-moving garden cart almost ran over Daddy and sent Mama and Brother Chili Bean diving into the bushes.

Me and those cabbages and carrots and 'taters and 'maters were soon swerving down the road like a snake in a cactus patch, gaining on Hester the mule and all that laundry faster than a cow could say moo to you, too. A regular flood of mishap, it was. Things were beginning to look kinda wild.

But wouldn't ya know! Things can *always* get wilder. I'd
plumb forgotten it was market day. Just as I reached rocket
ship speed, and was running within a curly hair's stretch of
Hester the mule, around the bend came little Sister Pinto Bean
and Grandpaw Bean in the farm truck, which was all loaded
up with apples.

Yep, wild indeedy, Ima Bean, I said to myself, and I knew for
sure it was true.

So I yelled at Grandpaw Bean that he'd plumb forgotten his fishing pole, and that I was just trying to help, but maybe he'd better get the farm truck out of the way before I explained it all.

Wouldn't ya know! He did just that.

Dear me. Oh my. Black clouds fly my troubles in the sky. I'd goofed.

So about then is when I decided to leave Mossyrock Creek for good. I bailed out of that garden cart—cabbages and carrots and 'taters and 'maters flying every whichaway—

ran fleahop fast back home through the woods, and packed my suitcase.

Gotta find a new family, Ima Bean, I said to myself. You've gone and broke Grandpaw Bean's fishing pole . . . and let Hester the mule out . . . and tore down Mama's clothes-line . . . and broke Brother Chili Bean's bike even worse than it was . . . and dumped those cabbages and carrots and 'taters and 'maters . . . and run Sister Pinto Bean and Grandpaw Bean and the family apples off the road. It's a terrible mess, a regular flood of mishap. No one will love you anymore.

Then I started to cry, 'cause I knew it was true.

But wouldn't ya know!

I'd plumb forgotten.

In my family, you're always family . . .
even when you goof!